I0559477

Dot Markers Animals Coloring Book for Kids Ages 1–5

Fun & Easy Bold Line Activities for Toddlers & Preschoolers | Boost Fine Motor Skills, Enhance Imagination & Creativity with Games | Scissor Practice, Maze Puzzles, Spelling, and Counting for Children

POLYMATH Panda

ISBN: 978-1-953149-79-4

This Book Belongs To:

_____

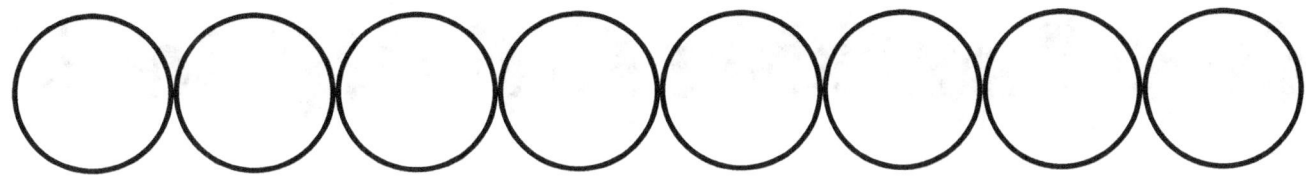

Grab Your Dot Markers and Dive into 50 Fun-Filled Pages of Cats, Dogs, Cows, and many more!

Featuring a wide variety of animals including Sheep, Dog, Alligator, Elephant, Chicken, and more. Includes engaging activities like Scissor Cutting, Counting, Mazes, Color Matching, and I Spy, all designed with large, easy-to-color dots. Perfectly compatible with all leading dot marker brands with consistent 0.75 inch (18mm) dots.

This book is a fantastic fit for young explorers aged 1 - 5. It's crafted to enhance your child's early learning journey with delightful animals designs that connect words, images, and colors. Our team of skilled designers has ensured each page stimulates your child's imagination and helps build their fine motor skills, making learning an exciting adventure!

We understand the enthusiasm of young dot marker artists, so we've designed each page to be single-sided, minimizing the risk of colors bleeding through. Additionally, placing a sheet of paper or card between the pages can be a great way to keep everything tidy!

Thank you for choosing this book! We hope it brings you and your child countless hours of dot marker joy and learning.

Free Printable Activity Book!

QR Code in the Back of the Book

- **Ignites Imagination:** Coloring with a story helps kids picture scenes and boost creativity.
- **Boosts Reading:** Following the story while coloring improves reading skills naturally.
- **Enhances Focus:** Storytelling with coloring keeps kids engaged and builds concentration.
- **Fosters Connection:** Coloring helps kids emotionally bond with characters and plots.
- **Fun Learning:** Makes learning enjoyable and easy through playful coloring.

Sheep

Spell out "Sheep" by dotting each letter

(S)　(h)　(e)　(e)　(p)

Week 1

Scissor Practice

Cut along the dotted line to practice your scissor skills.

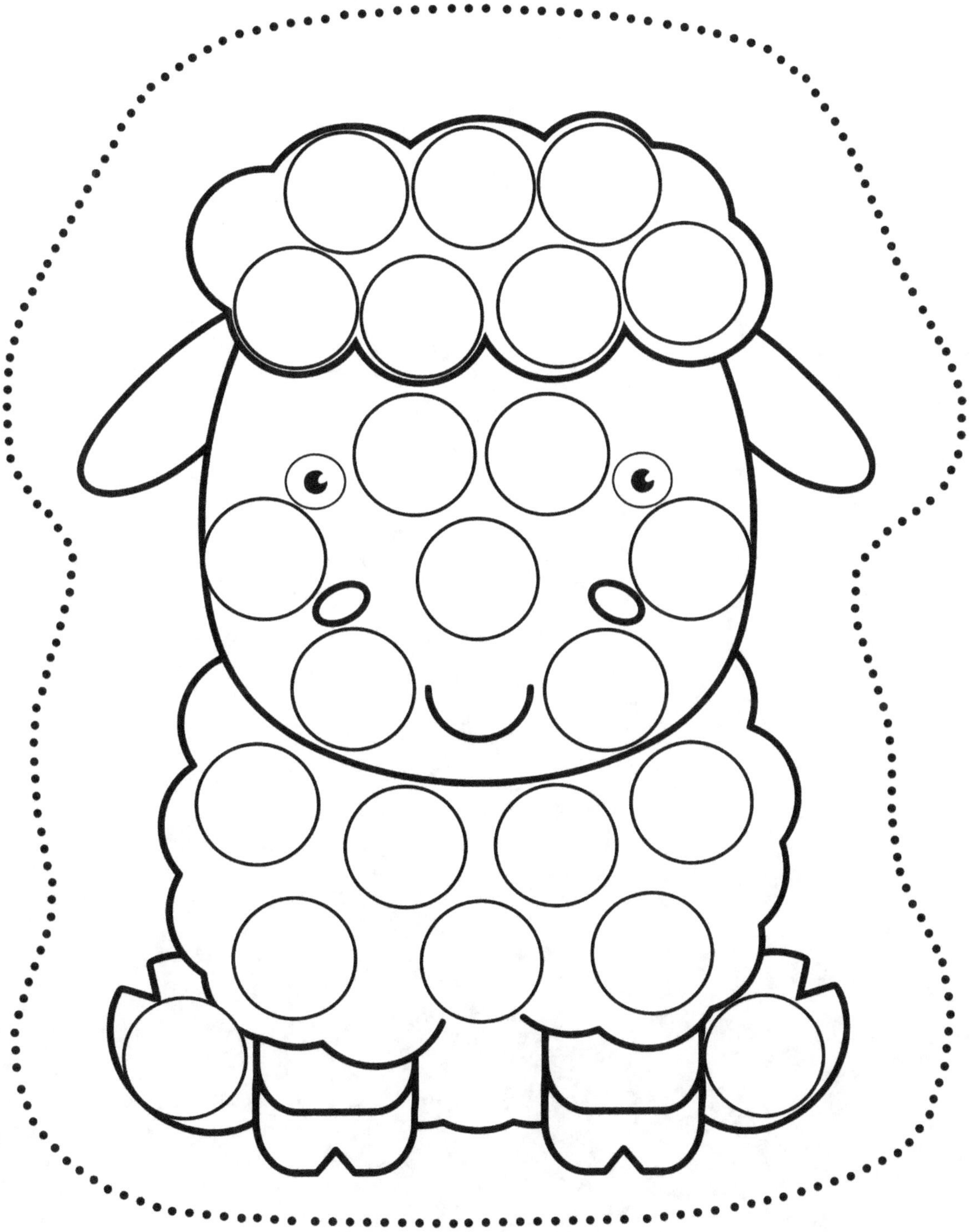

I Spy

 **I SPY** **Find the Sheep and dot it.**

Week 1

Maze

Dot the circles to help the farmer find the sheep.

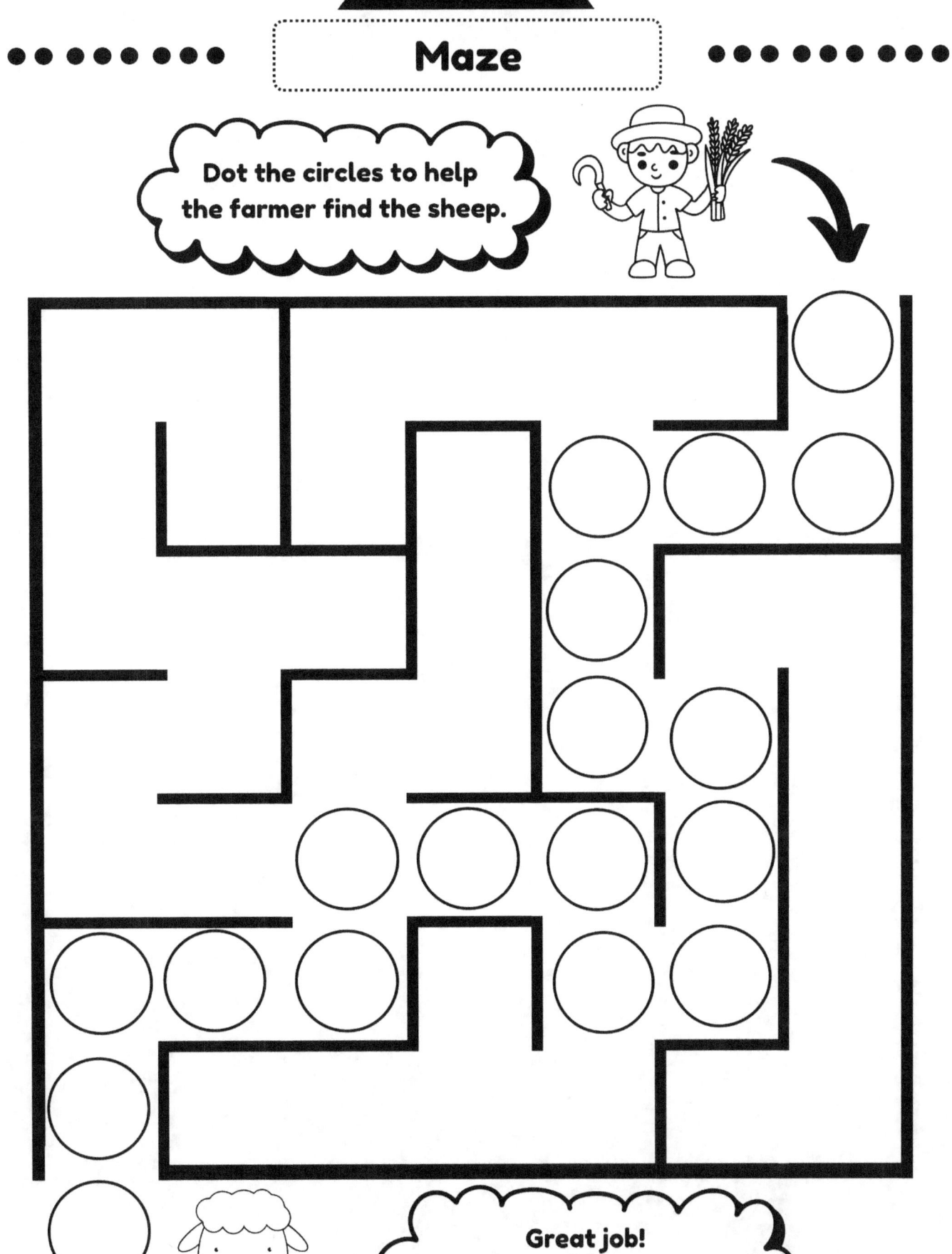

Great job!
The farmer found the sheep!

4

Lion

Spell out "Lion" by dotting each letter

(L) (i) (o) (n)

5

Week 2

Scissor Practice

Cut along the dotted line to practice your scissor skills.

Color Match

Dot all Lions Red

Dot all Sheep Blue

Counting

Dot 3 Lions

Dot 2 Sheep

Rabbit

Spell out "Rabbit" by dotting each letter

(R) (a) (b) (b) (i) (t)

Scissor Practice

Cut along the dotted line to practice your scissor skills.

I Spy

I SPY Find the Rabbit and dot it.

Dot the circles to help the rabbit find its home

Fantastic!
The Rabbit found its home!

Tiger

Spell out "Tiger" by dotting each letter

(T)   (i)   (g)   (e)   (r)

Cut along the dotted line to practice your scissor skills.

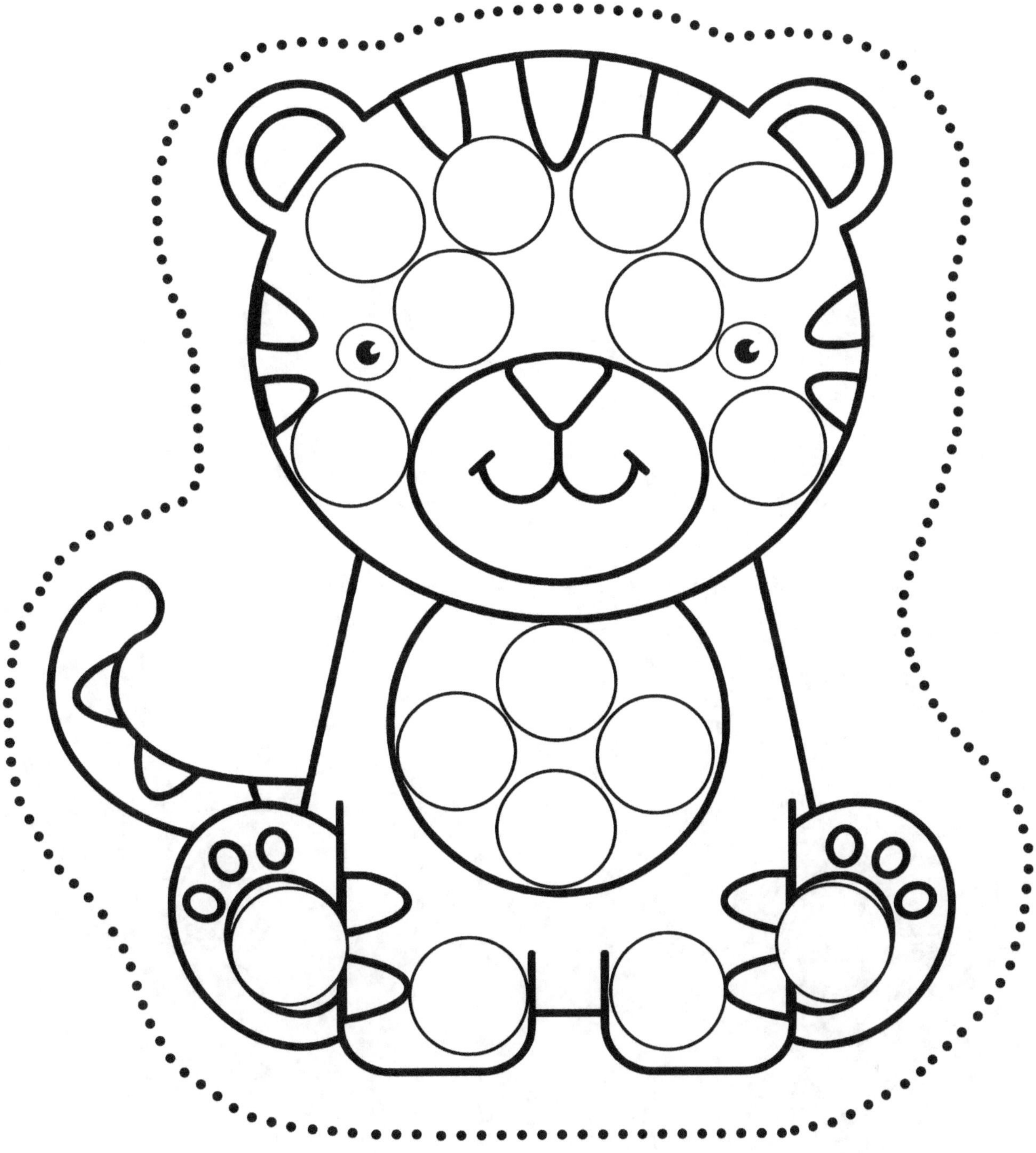

Week 4

Color Match

 **Dot all Tigers Violet**

 **Dot all Rabbits Orange**

15

Counting

Dot 4 Tigers

Dot 2 Rabbits

Monkey

Spell out "Monkey" by dotting each letter

M   o   n   k   e   y

Week 5

Scissor Practice

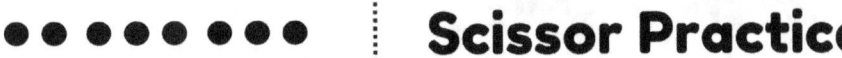

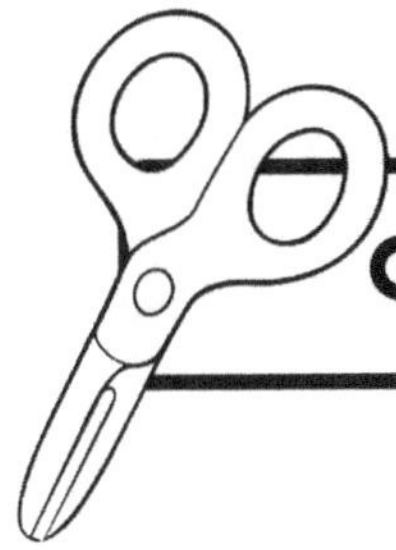

Cut along the dotted line to practice your scissor skills.

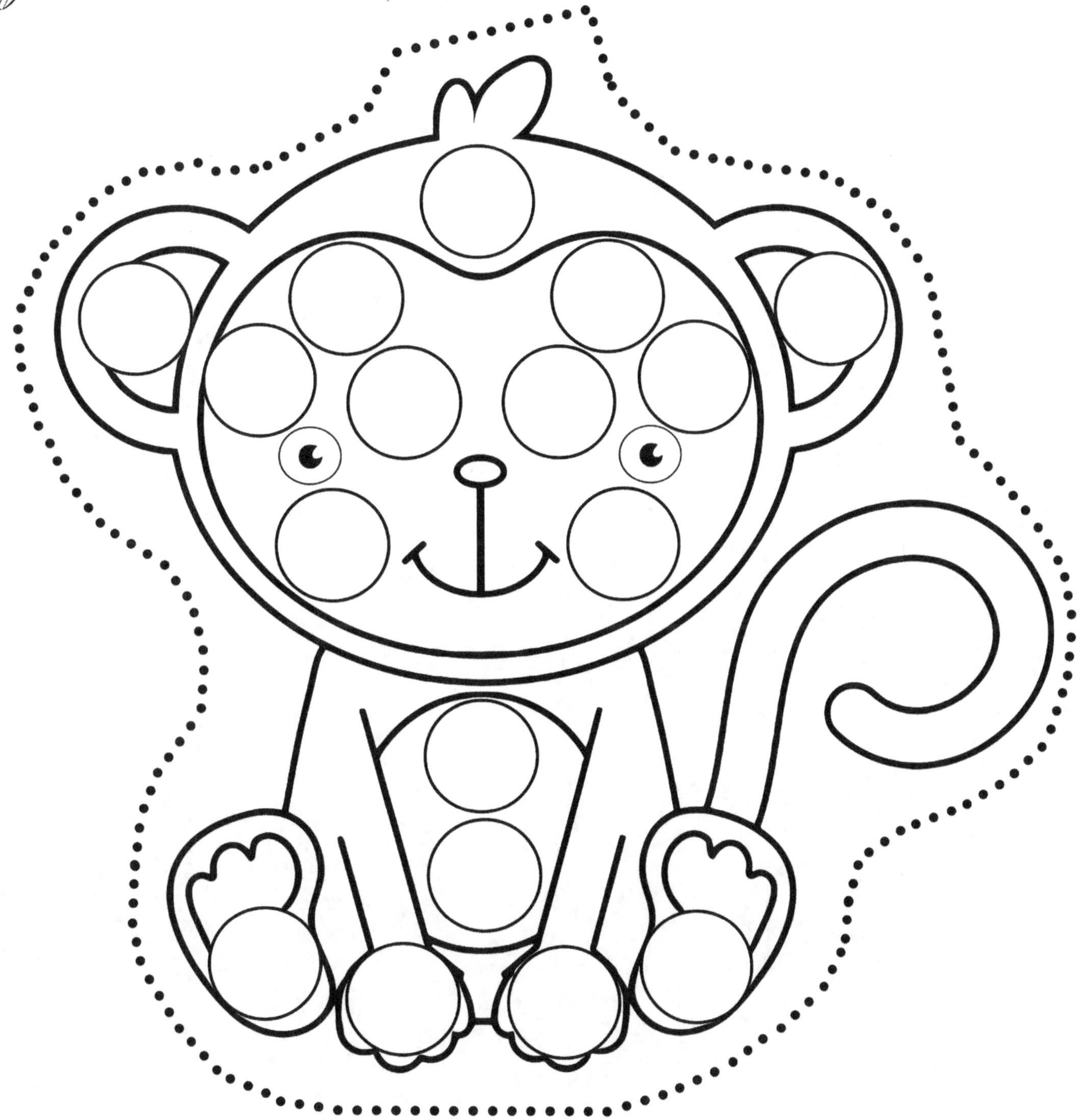

I Spy

 Find the Monkey and dot it.

Maze

Dot the circles to help the monkey find the banana!

Nicely done!
The Monkey found the banana!

Crocodile

Spell out "Crocodile" by dotting each letter

C   r   o   c   o   d   i   l   e

Week 6

Scissor Practice

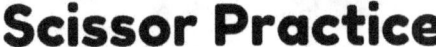

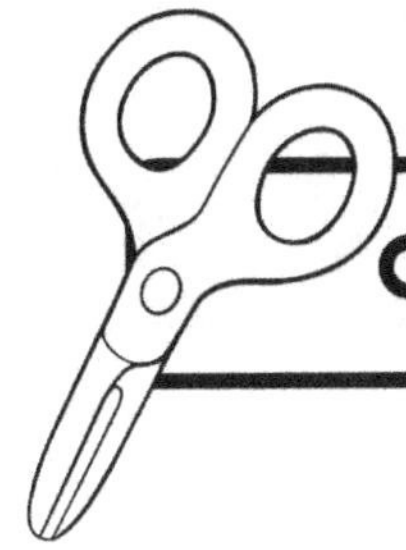

Cut along the dotted line to practice your scissor skills.

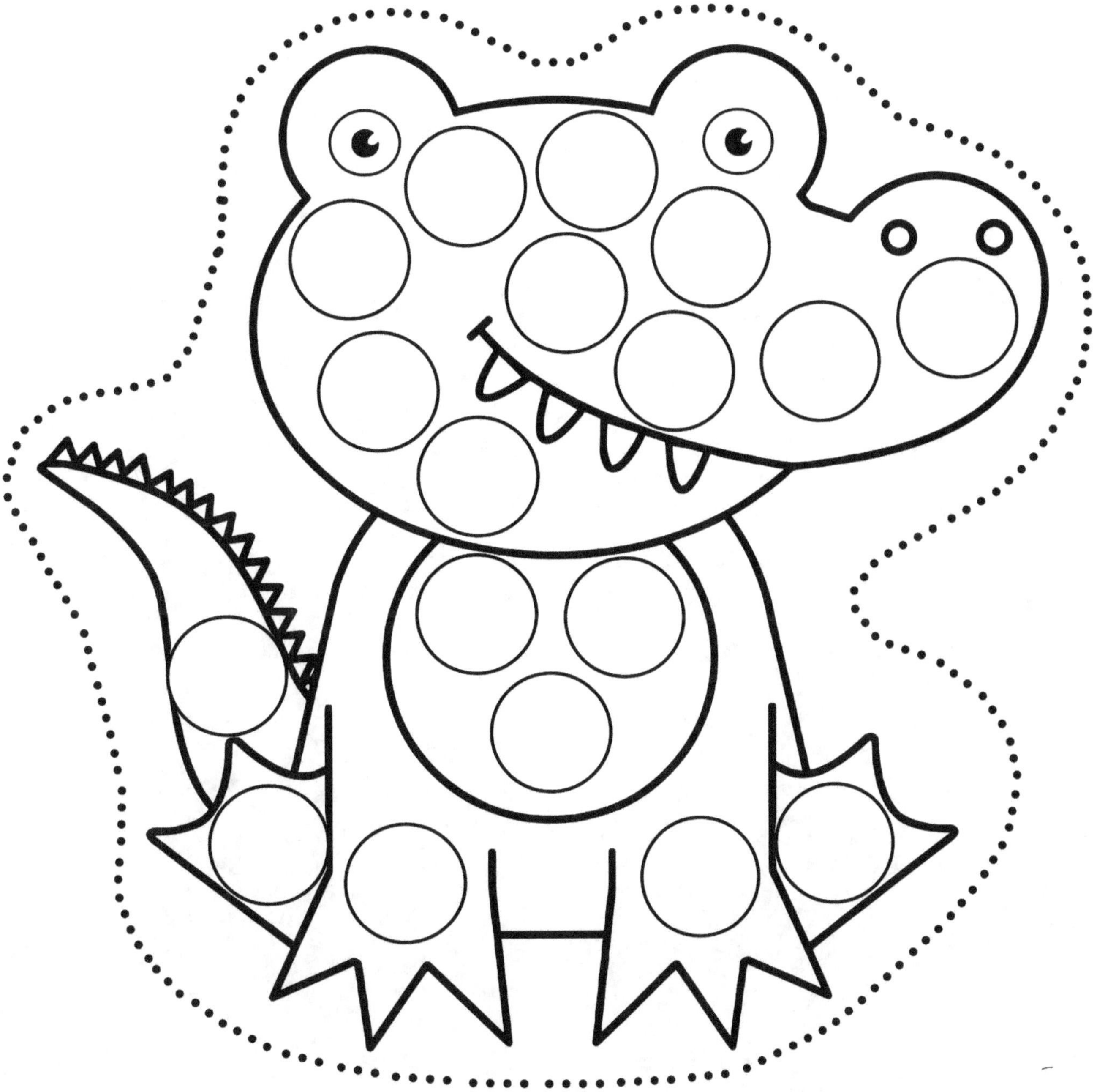

Dot all Crocodiles Orange

Dot all Monkeys Blue

Counting

Dot 1 Crocodile

Dot 3 Monkeys

Dog

Spell out "Dog" by dotting each letter

D o g

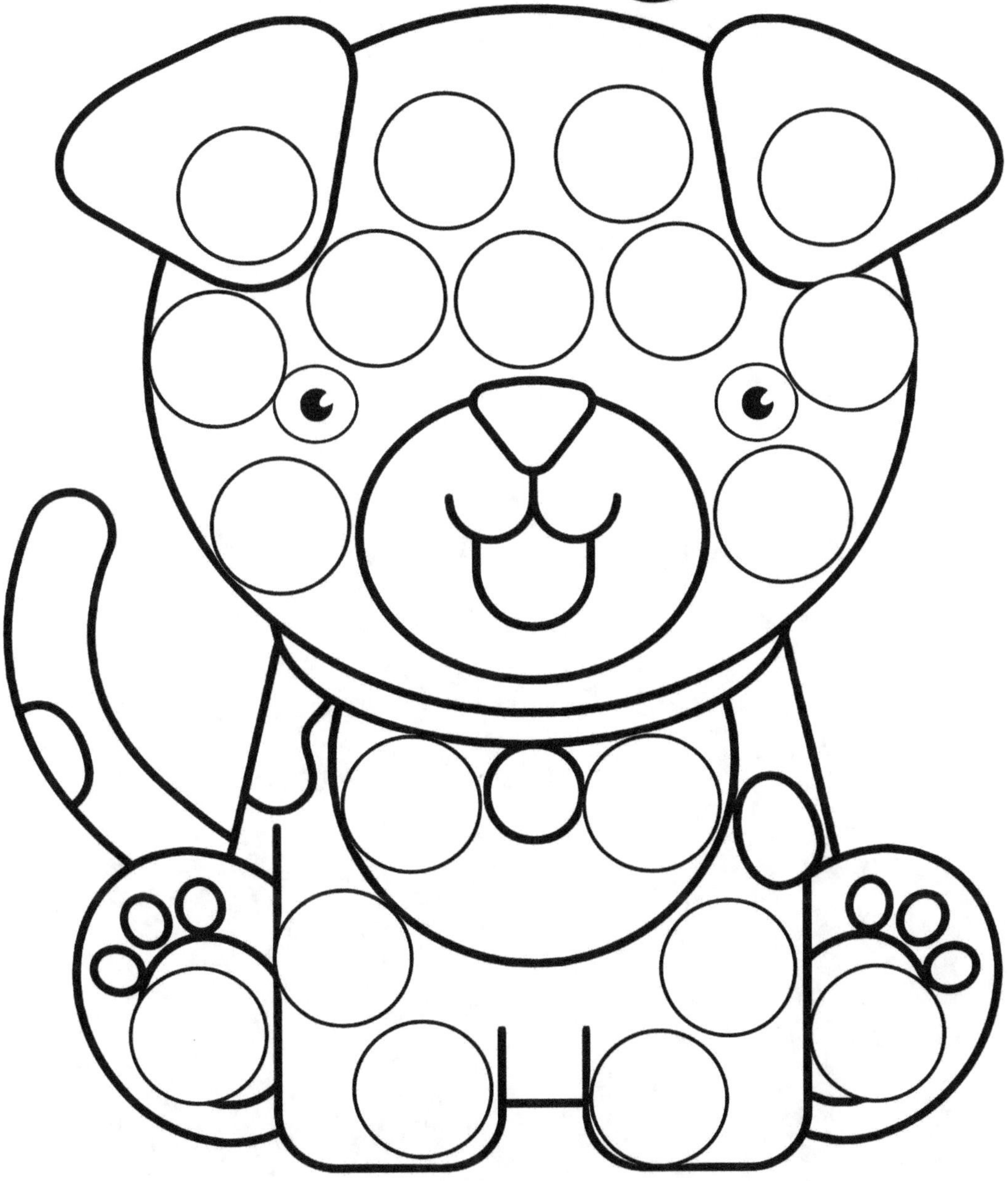

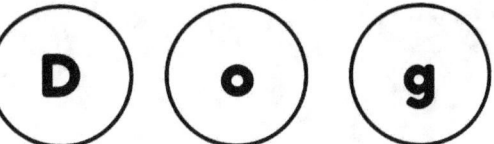

Week 7

Scissor Practice

Cut along the dotted line to practice your scissor skills.

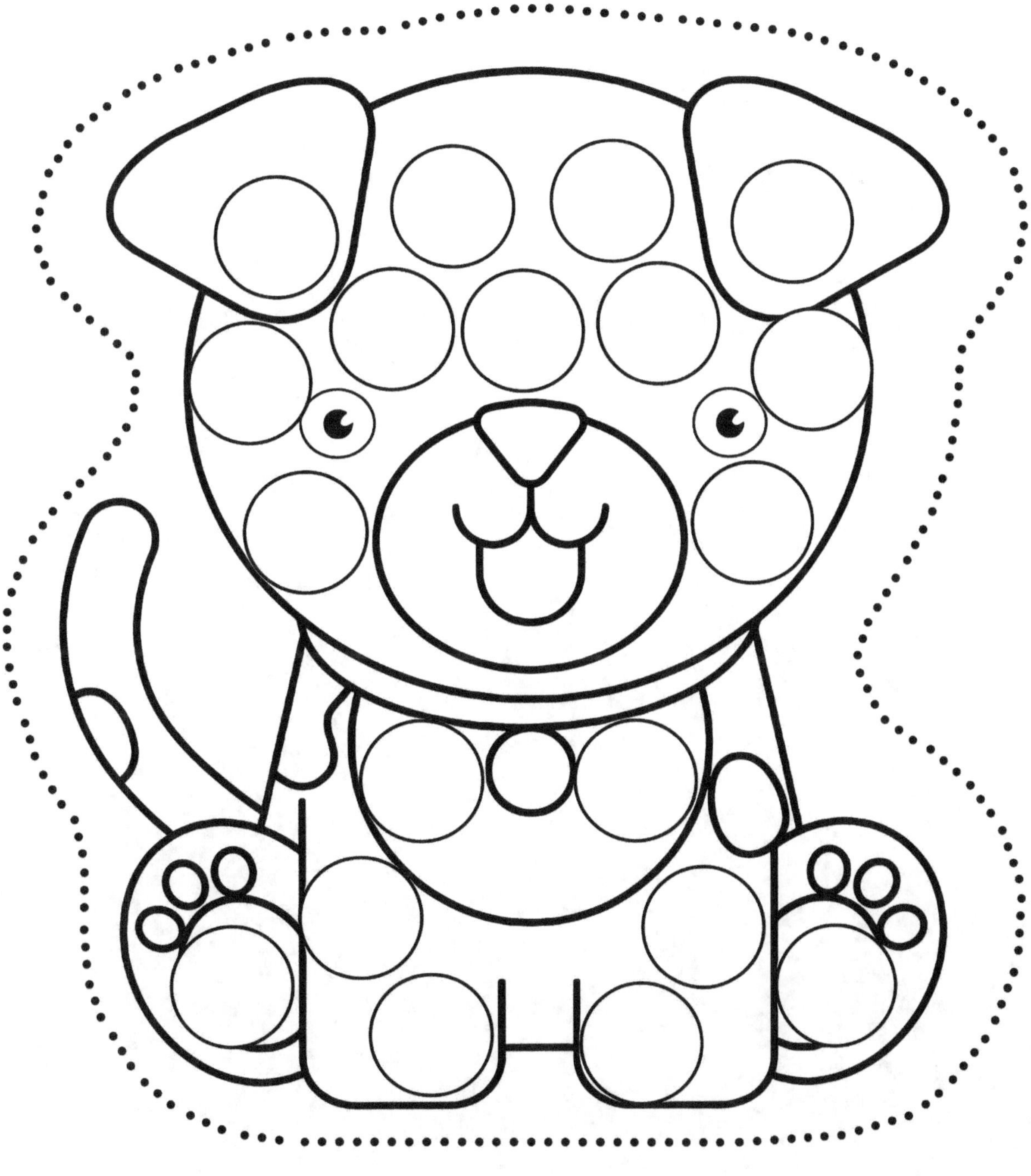

I Spy

I SPY | **Find the Dog and dot it.**

Maze

Dot the circles to help Molly find her dog.

Awesome!
Molly found her dog!

Elephant

Spell out "Elephant" by dotting each letter

E   l   e   p   h   a   n   t

Scissor Practice

Cut along the dotted line to practice your scissor skills.

Color Match

 **Dot all Dogs Green**

 **Dot all Elephants Red**

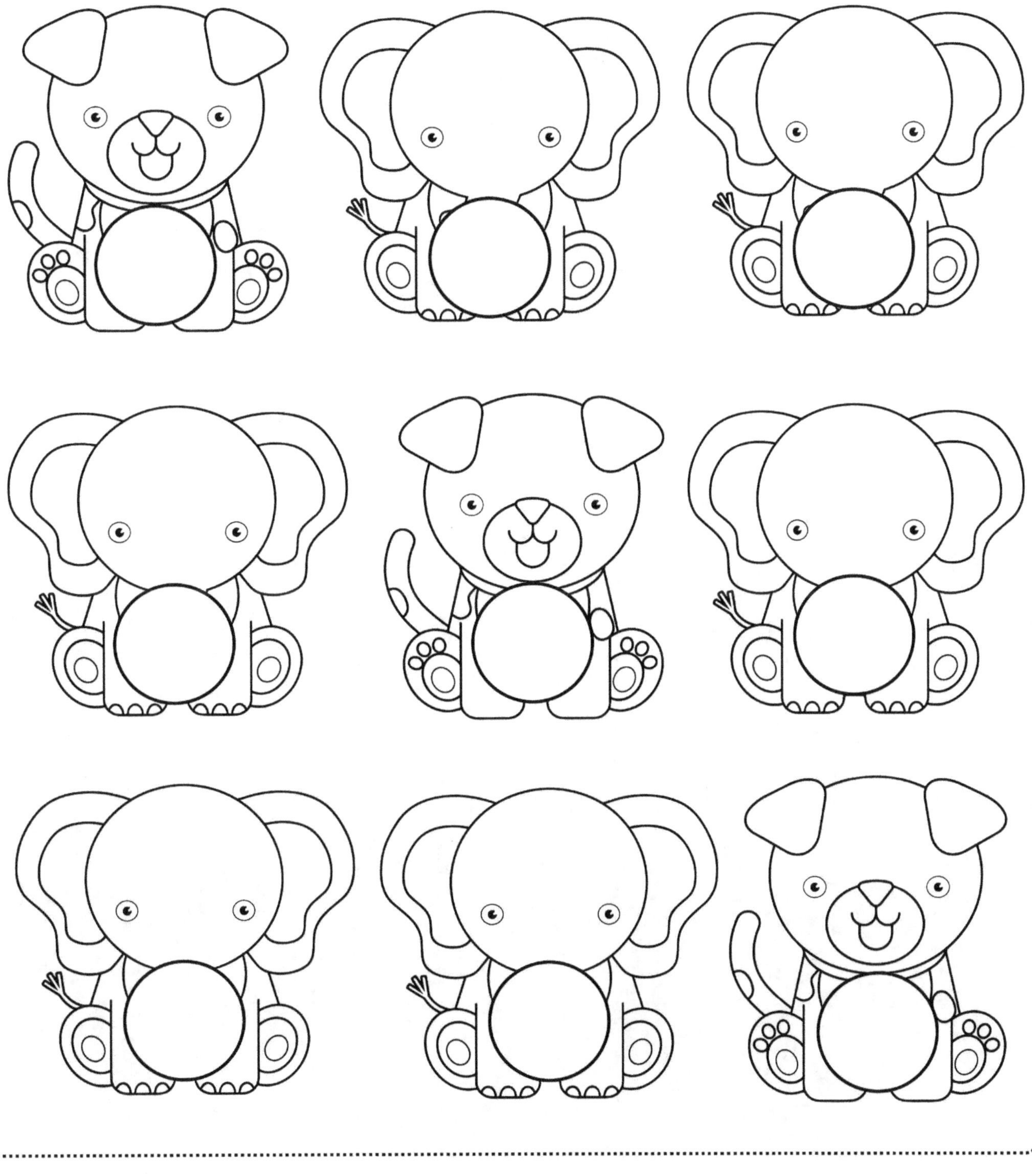

Counting

Dot 1 Dog

Dot 3 Elephants

 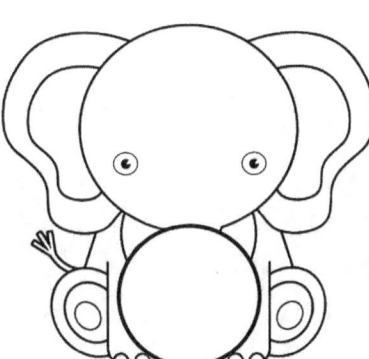 

Cow

Spell out "Cow" by dotting each letter

(C) (o) (w)

Week 9

Scissor Practice

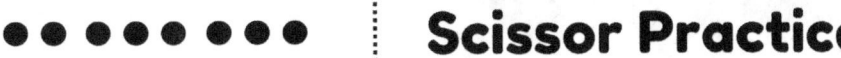

Cut along the dotted line to practice your scissor skills.

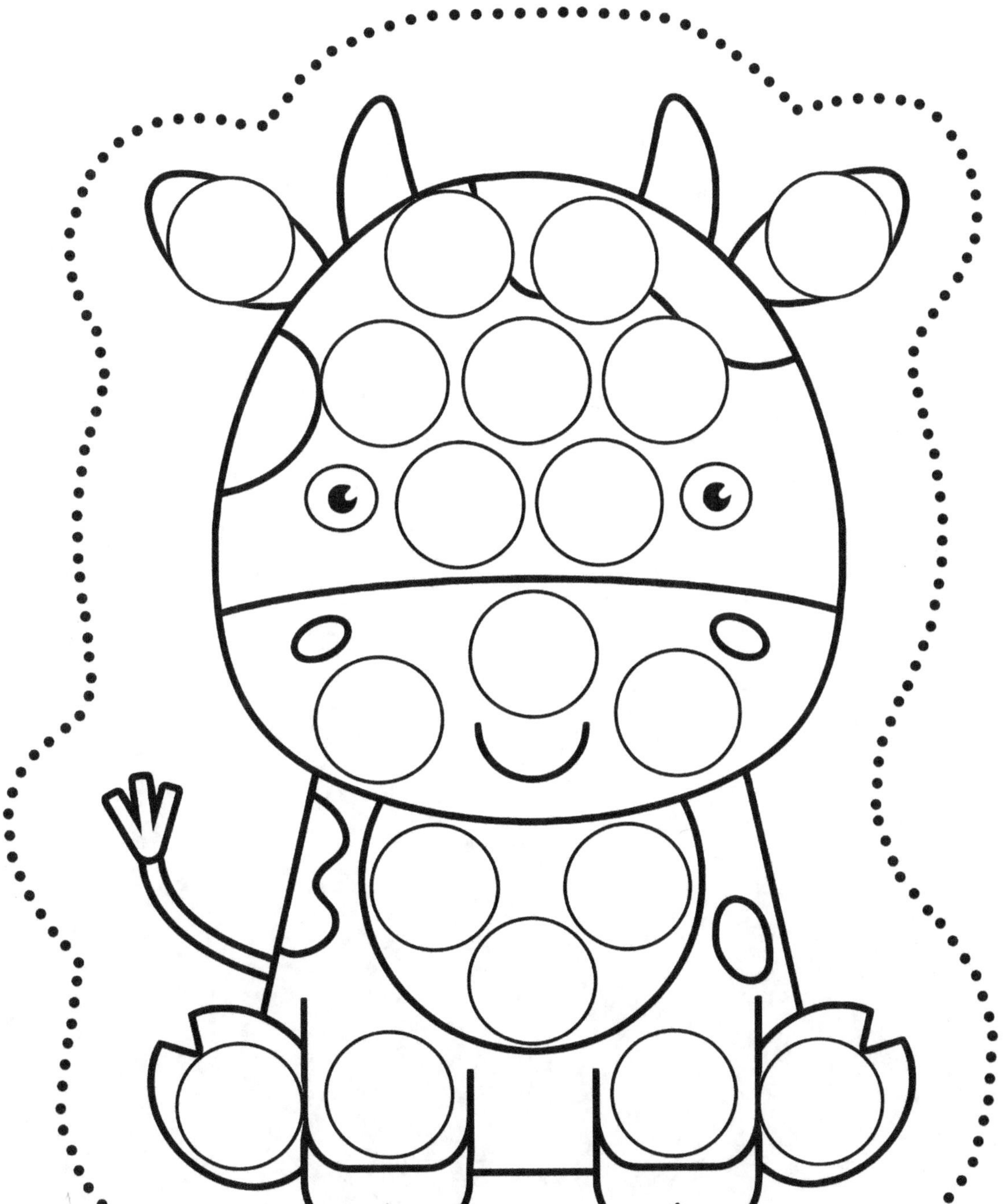

I Spy

I SPY Find the Cow and dot it.

Maze

Dot the circles to help the cow find the grass!

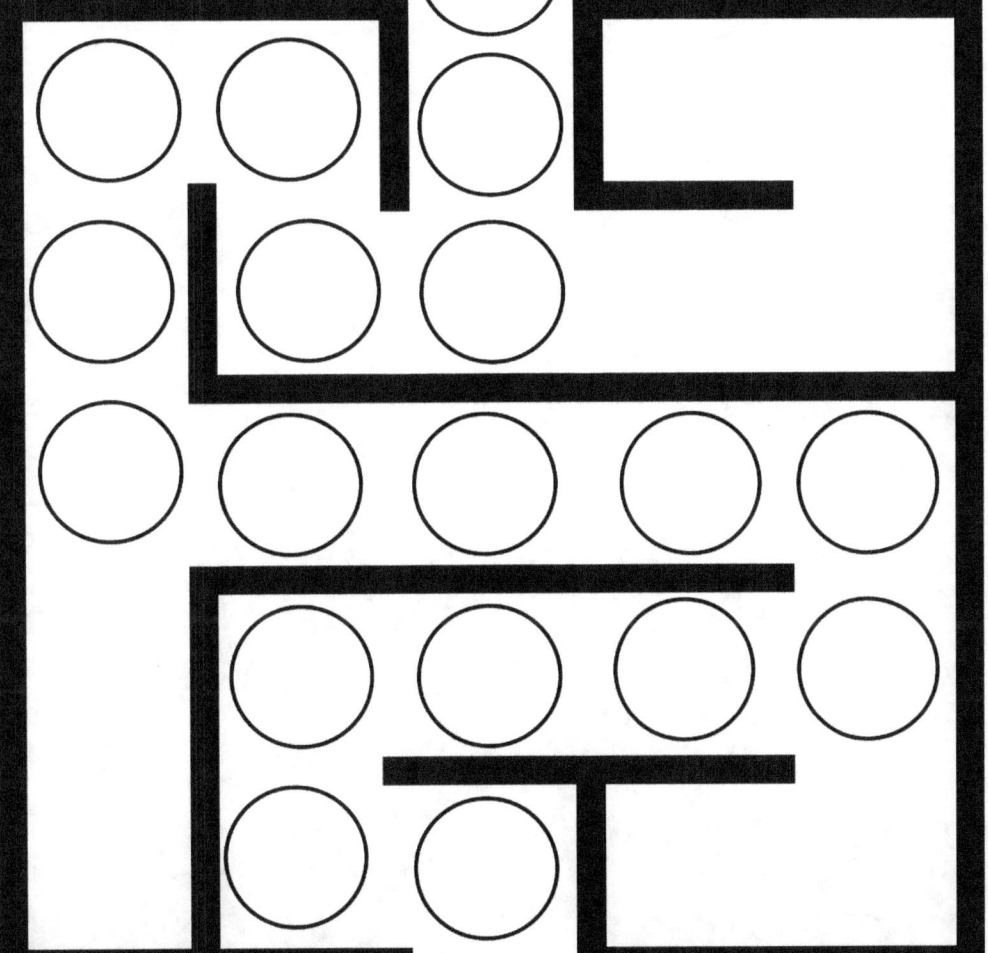

Well done!
The cow found the grass!

Chicken

Spell out "Chicken" by dotting each letter

(C)   (h)   (i)   (c)   (k)   (e)   (n)

Cut along the dotted line to practice your scissor skills.

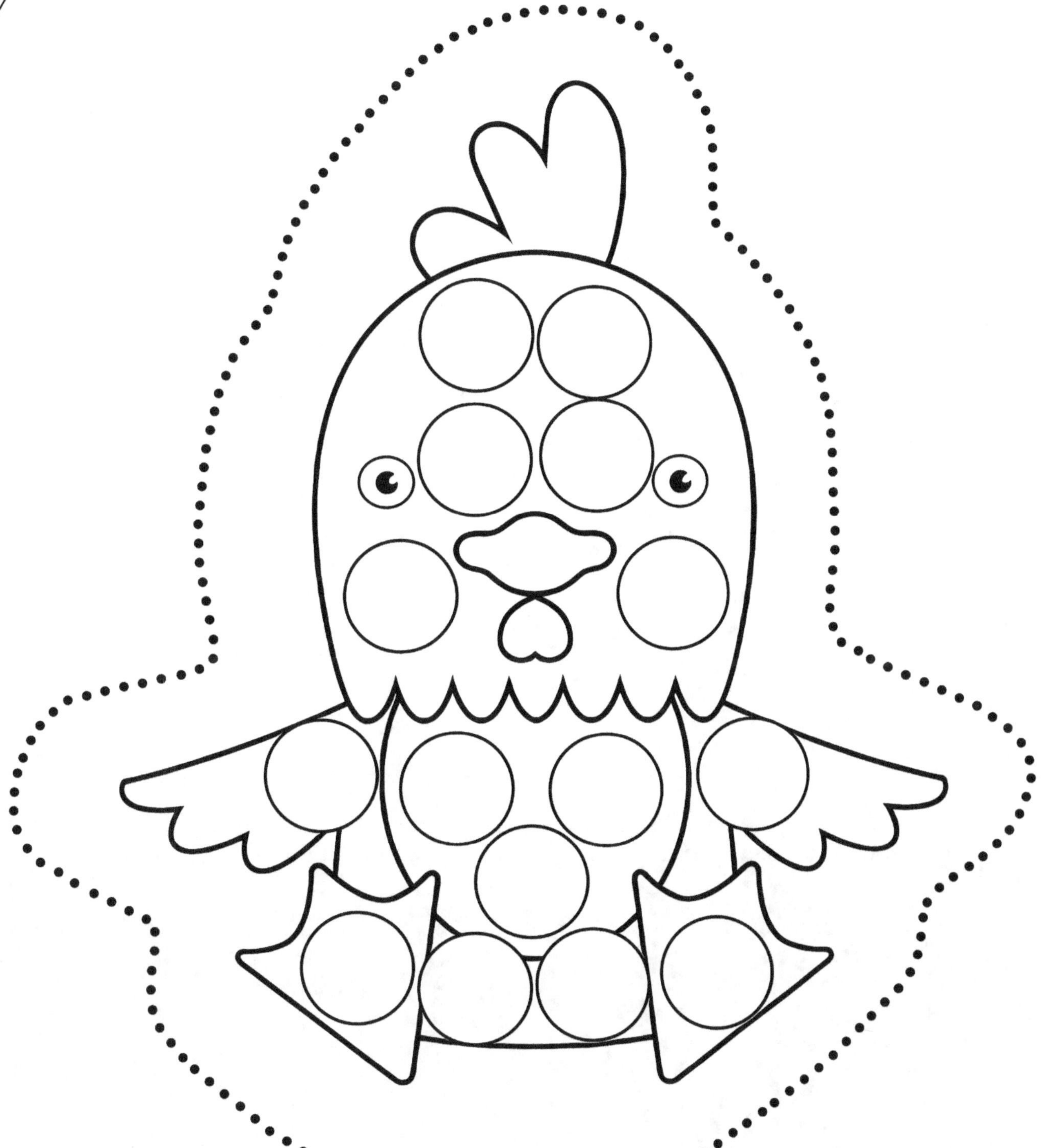

Color Match

Dot all Chickens Yellow

Dot all Cows Orange

Counting

Dot 4 Chickens

Dot 3 Cows

Cat

Spell out "Cat" by dotting each letter

C   a   t

Week 11

Scissor Practice

Cut along the dotted line to practice your scissor skills.

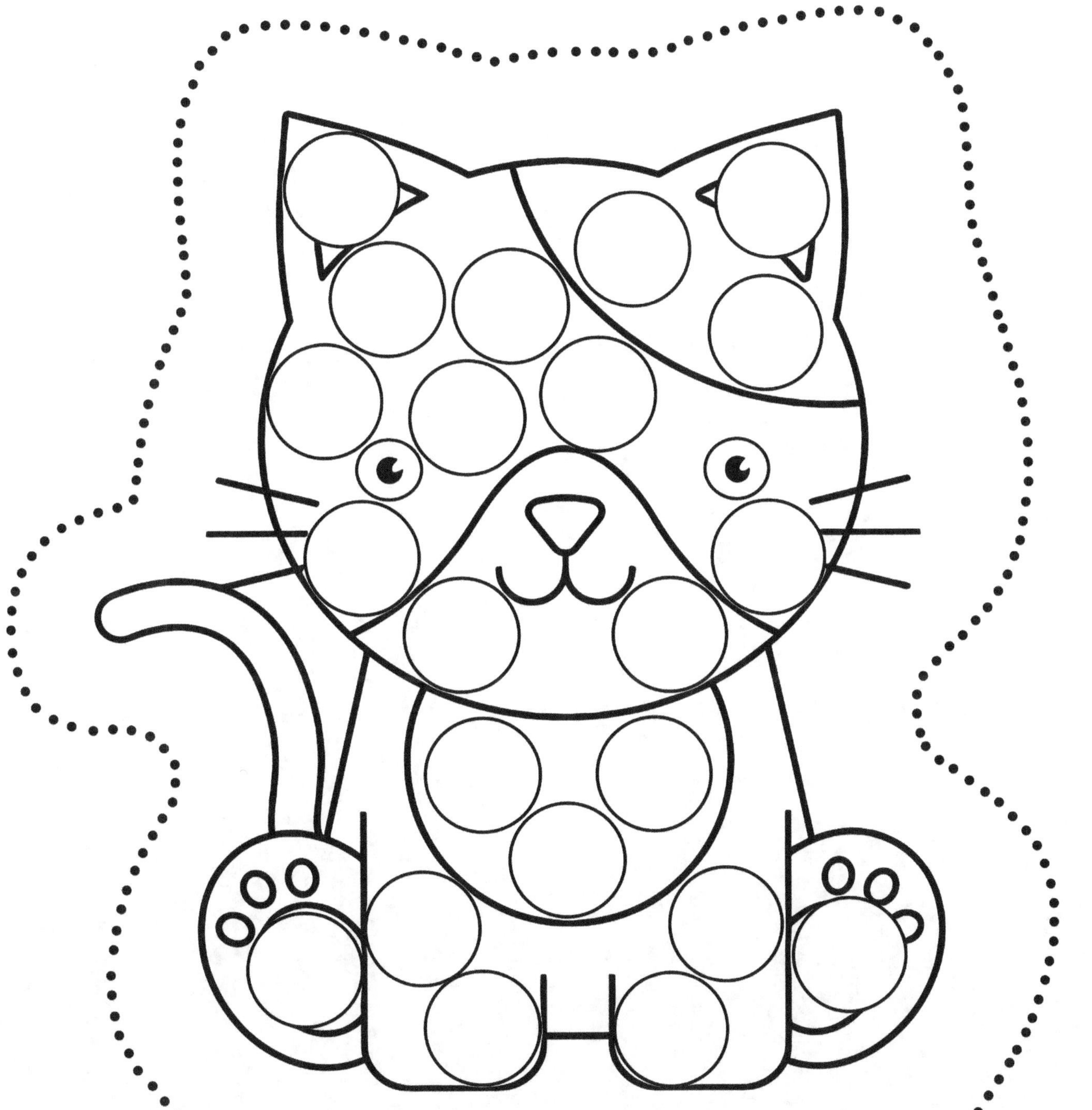

I Spy

I SPY Find the Cat and dot it.

Maze

Dot the circles to help Joshua find his cat.

Great!
Joshua found his cat!

Seal

Spell out "Seal" by dotting each letter

(S)   (e)   (a)   (l)

Week 12

Scissor Practice

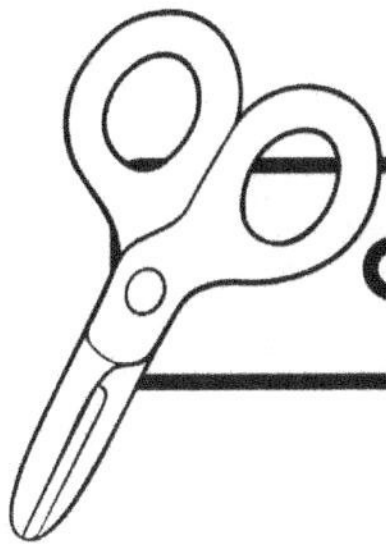

Cut along the dotted line to practice your scissor skills.

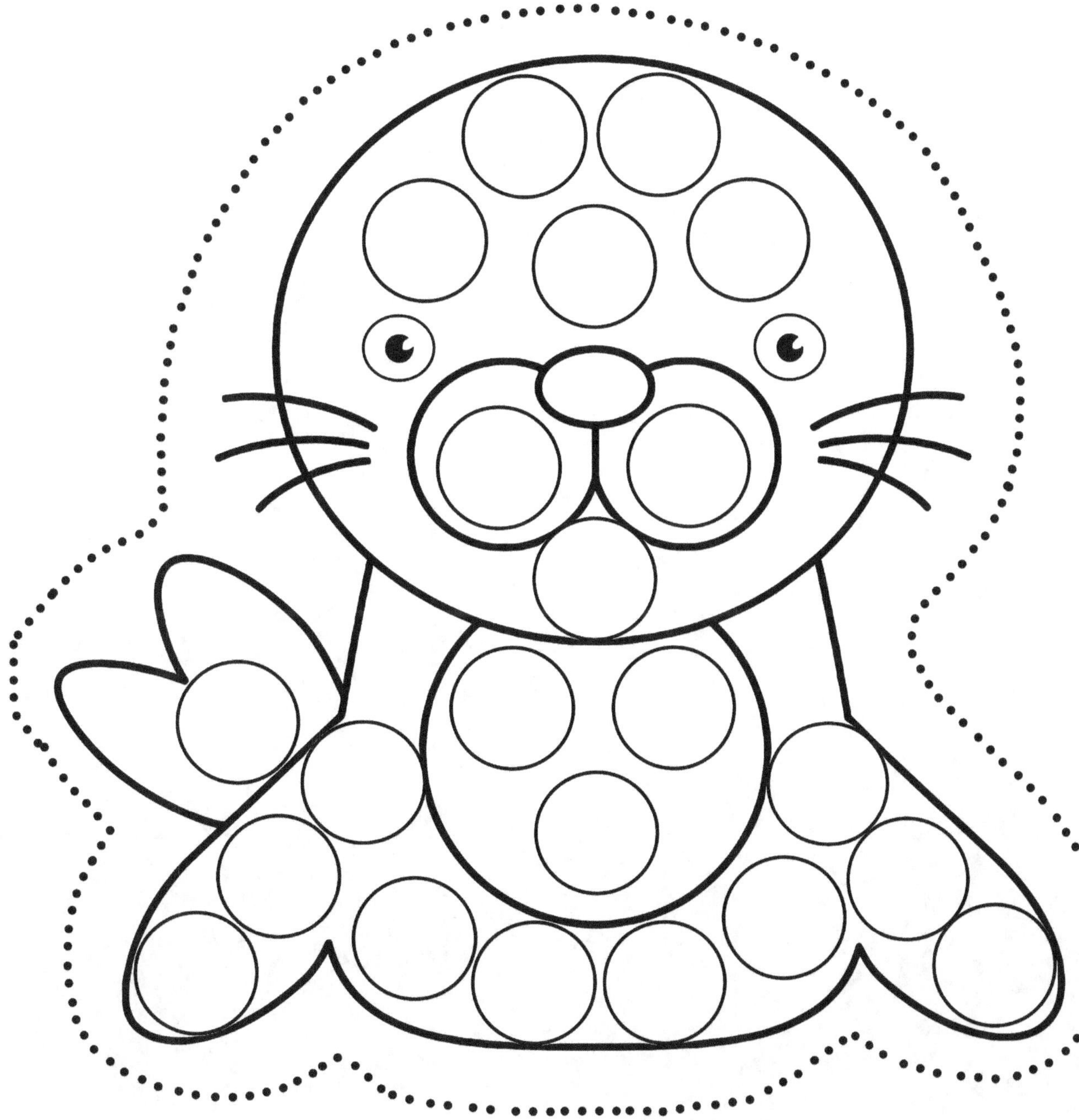

Color Match

Dot all Cats Orange

Dot all Seals Green

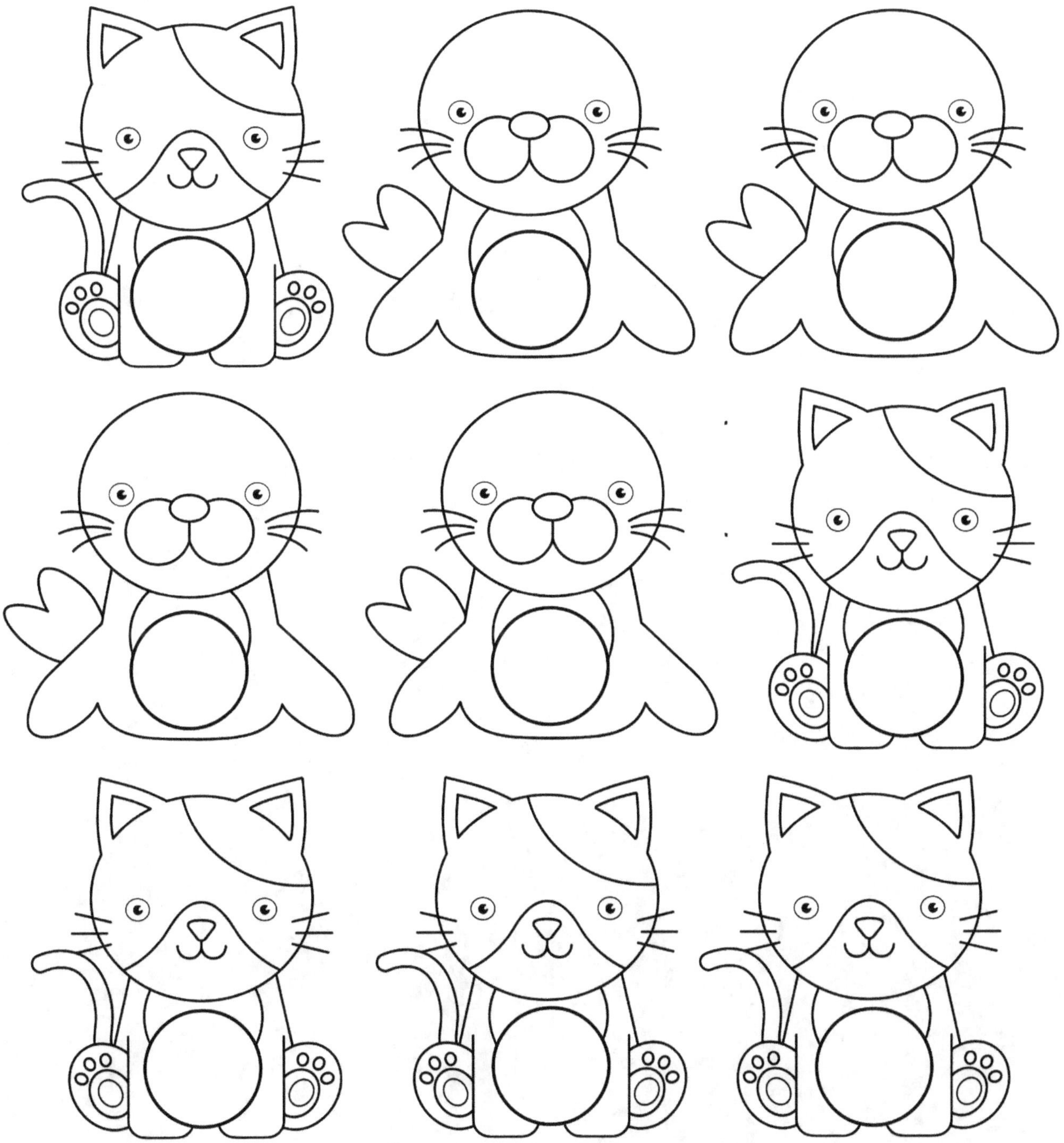

Counting

Dot 5 Seals

Dot 2 Cats

Rhino

Spell out "Rhino" by dotting each letter

(R) (h) (i) (n) (o)

Cut along the dotted line to practice your scissor skills.

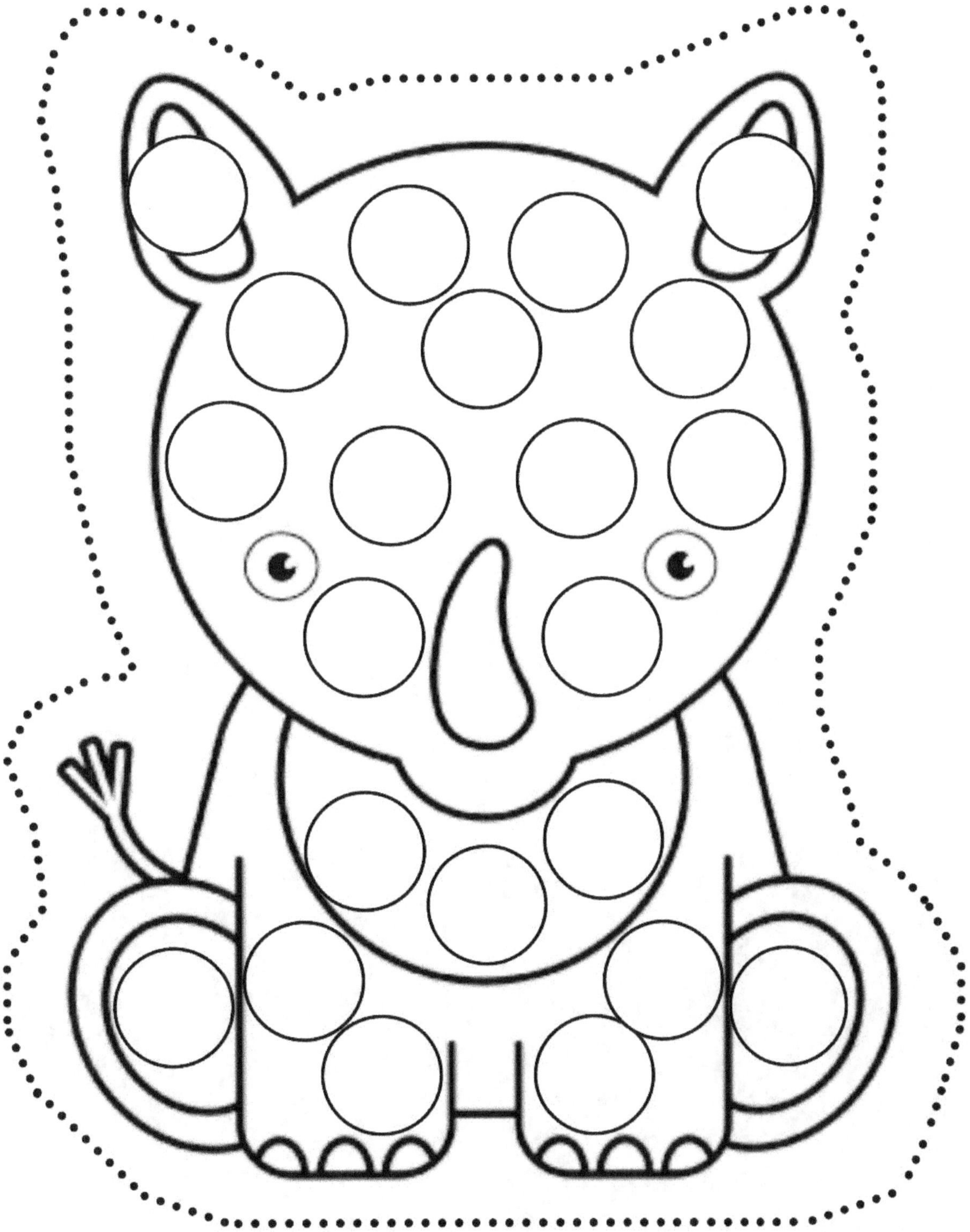

I Spy

 **Find the rhino and dot it.**

Maze

Dot the circles to help the rhino find the Tree.

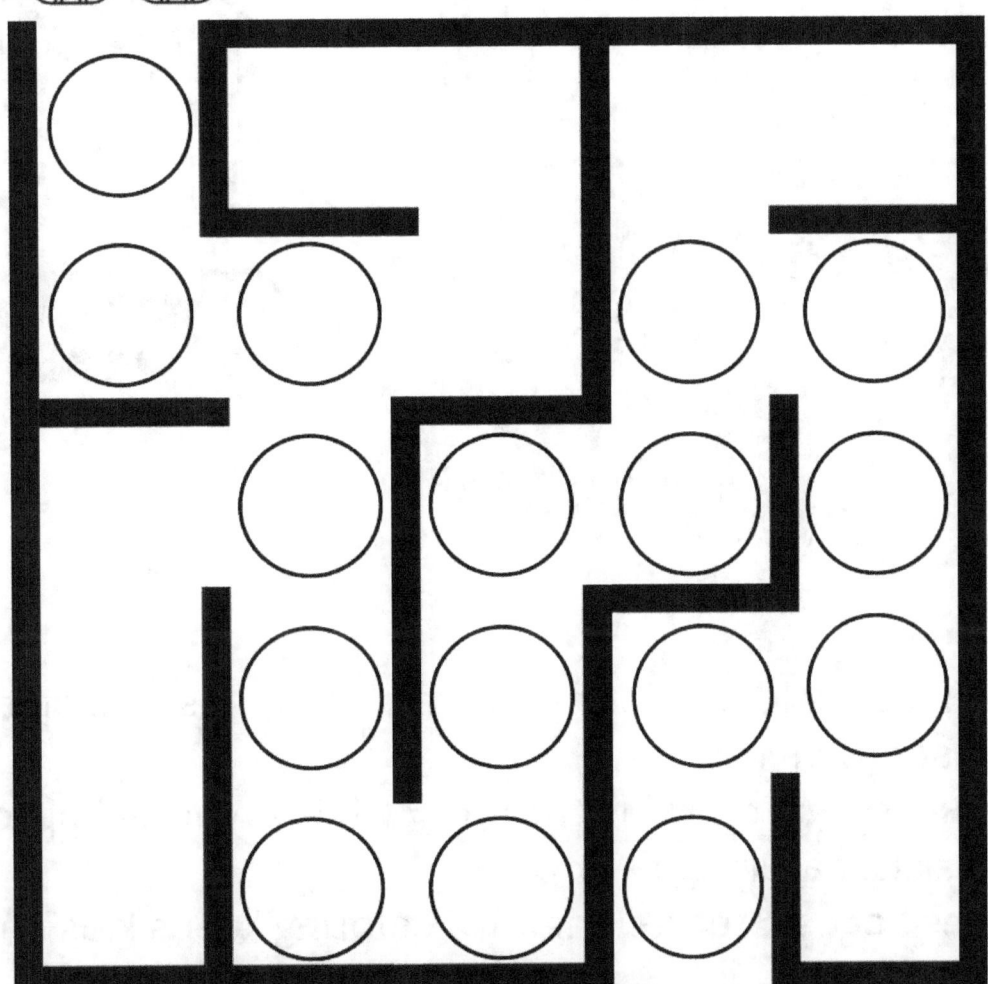

Great!
The rhino found its tree!

Free Printable Activity Book!

- **Ignites Imagination:** Coloring with a story helps kids picture scenes and boost creativity.
- **Boosts Reading:** Following the story while coloring improves reading skills naturally.
- **Enhances Focus:** Storytelling with coloring keeps kids engaged and builds concentration.
- **Fosters Connection:** Coloring helps kids emotionally bond with characters and plots.
- **Fun Learning:** Makes learning enjoyable and easy through playful coloring.

Parents & Teachers!

Our biggest joy comes from helping little ones flourish and discover the world around them through learning.

That's why your thoughts matter so much to us!

Your honest thoughts about our book, even a quick sentence or two, would mean the world. We really mean it!

You'd be making a big difference for a small education brand like ours, run with love by a mother-daughter team.

Your reviews help us reach more curious minds across the globe, paving their way to success in their educational journey.

And hey, maybe we'll even sell a few more books in the process!

Every single review makes our hearts swell with gratitude.

Ready to make our day?

Scan the QR Code below to share your thoughts.

www.ingramcontent.com/pod-product-compliance
Lightning Source LLC
Chambersburg PA
CBHW081004120626
46546CB00010B/3007